The Isthmus of Samuel Greenberg

Shearsman Library Vol. 6

The Isthmus of

Jeremy Reed

Samuel Greenberg

Shearsman Library

Second Edition.
Published in the United Kingdom in 2018 by
Shearsman Library
an imprint of Shearsman Books
by Shearsman Books Ltd
50 Westons Hill Drive
Emersons Green
BRISTOL
BS16 7DF

Shearsman Books Ltd Registered Office
30–31 St. James Place, Mangotsfield, Bristol BS16 9JB
(this address not for correspondence)

www.shearsman.com

ISBN 978-1-84861-590-8

First published by Trigram Press, London, 1976

Foggy Days

I grew up in a foggy teal-blue bubble, facing out into the hazy waters of the Gulf of St Malo on the north coast of Jersey, and the English Channel on the south, the iridescent dissolve of sea into sky filtered into everything I wrote, as a sort of fuzzy molecular glow. I was offshore, off-world, part of the Îles de la Manche, the remnants of the Duchy of Normandy. Totally supportive from my early teens that I should just write, and pursue no other future, my mother encouraged me in what I formatively wrote as a schoolboy, most often sitting out alone on deserted beaches, bought me random anthologies of modern poetry. Through accidental reading I discovered the elusive, metaphorically dense poems of Hart Crane, rinsed with hallucinated sea-imagery, and built out of what seemed the collision of a coded sexuality with big city life pushed to extremes, as though its author in the process of attempting to overtake himself was sent propulsively back from the future into the crisis of the present. My enthusiasm for Crane led to my mother ordering me his *Collected Poems*, the 1968 OUP edition, with a compelling Walker Evans photo of Hart Crane, dissolutely staring from the jacket, his hair prematurely silvered at thirty, the rashed vesicles on his face pointing to what I was to learn later was his incurable alcoholism. I was quickly absorbed into the Crane mythology, intensified in my mind by his spectacularly heroic suicide in jumping from the stern of the *SS Orizaba* into the Gulf of Mexico, dead at noon on 27 April 1932. The image of his unrecovered body orbited my hyperactive imagination as I hung out, moody, confused, needing to get away from Jersey, but at the same time polarised to my own local seas morphing through every variant of blue, green and grey, according to the seasonally interfacing sky.

The love of Crane's romantically enthused, dynamically energised poetry took me out of curiosity to his letters as a biographical resource to enhancing my understanding of the poems. It was there I encountered the name of a little-known poet, Samuel Greenberg, who died of aggressive tuberculosis at the age of 23 on August 17, 1917, at the Sea View Hospital on Staten Island. Crane, who compared Greenberg to the likes of Rimbaud, had read his poems in manuscript form and picked up on dazzling verbal clusters that connected with his own electrifying impulse to write poetry as new.

Alienated, head full of David Bowie's Ziggy Stardust, as identifiable alien humanoid, and writing afternoons at the low-life Harbour Café, I began this sequential poem in the attempt to integrate my own local geography into the lives of Hart Crane and Samuel Greenberg, working no differently to how I do today, with a sign pen and lined notebook. And not knowing what to do with my work, and having for some time dosed up on his romantically transgressive elegies, I decided impulsively to send a packet of my juvenilia, including *Isthmus* to George Barker, care of his publishers. To my astonishment, George replied, telling me how much he liked the poems and that I'd 'clearly been bitten in the calf by the Muse,' and that he was sending my poems on to Asa Benveniste of Trigram Press, who had published a recent book of his, *At Thurgarton Church*. George also suggested I visited him at his home in the tiny village of Itteringham in Norfolk, and 'that together we should throw salt over the Devil's tail'.

Some weeks later I received a letter written in China black ink on Trigram-headed cream handmade paper from Asa Ben-veniste, comparing my Crane-influenced pyrotechnical start-outs to Rimbaud, and telling me that not only did he want to publish a book by me, but that he was very fortuitously visiting Jersey for two days to stay with Michael Armstrong, who was considering buying into Trigram as a partner, and that he very much wanted to meet me. Three weeks later, the two came to my mother's house, Asa dressed head-to-toe in black: black shirt, black jeans, black Chelsea boots, his right hand a fist of cloudy moonstones and opals. Thin, maybe 140lbs, chain-smoking Camels, wired, his voice sharing affinities with Leonard Cohen, Asa brought me a packet of Trigram books, Tom Raworth's *Big Green Day* and *Lion Lion*, Nathaniel Tarn's *October*, his own *AtoZ*

Formula, George Barker's *At Thurgarton Church*, all in his own beautifully idiosyncratic designs, to help me try get acquainted with the new modalities of poetry. He suggested at first he publish a book of thirty of my poems to be called *Neurocans in Deserted Swimming Pools*, but later decided he would start with *The Isthmus of Samuel Greenberg*, choosing sea greens and purple for the cover, and a photo of the Statue of Liberty, as a thrown allusion to Hart Crane having lived at Columbia Heights looking out over the harbours, and waiting for drunken wedges of sailors to disembark and fill the dockside bars. In addition, Asa guided me towards doing a degree in American poetry at the University of Essex to help liberate me from Jersey's inhibitive, cultureless milieu, and as the first step towards coming to live permanently in London.

American poetry was so much ahead of its conservative British counterpart; Ed Dorn, John Wieners, Robert Duncan, John Ashbery, Frank O'Hara, James Schuyler, all injected an imaginative, image-driven, freed-up schematic into a poetry contemporaneous with change, rather than working backwards, which was how I saw most British poetry, with the exception of J.H. Prynne and his alumni, who were crunched into a cryptic language prism. Being a student at Essex also allowed me to visit Asa regularly at his Leverton Street house in Kentish Town, where, growing progressively disillusioned with publishing – he used to complain there was nobody he wanted to publish – and with his marriage to Pip disintegrating, he was often resorting to drinking a bottle of scotch a day, starting sometimes at 10 a.m. and continuing to drink steadily through the day. He'd accepted for publication a 200-page poem of mine called *Logoin* – I suspect the manuscript is lost – but lacked the funding to bring this out, or the later books he'd contracted. He was to honour the dying Louis Zukofsky's *A 22 and 23* as his final serious Trigram commitment.

With Asa caring little for distribution, outside of Compendium, Bernard Stone and Foyles, most of the later Trigram titles, including mine, joined the long queue of missing books retrieved only by a dedicated cult. Asa largely took the view that the sort of poetry he published migrated in time to the right readers. He was a serious adept of Kabbala and believed in the motivations of magic and synchronicity, and that poetry was an active part of that intuitive process.

I haven't read *The Isthmus of Samuel Greenberg* since I wrote it, mostly in a shabby harbour café, where two store thieves would meet regularly over tea and compare each other's tacky shoplifting for the day. There was always a smell of distance and sea fog in the air, and to me it became associated with the sniff of the future that was already happening in the moment of realising it. I was trying to travel with it and this little book happened along the way, and outside it always seemed to be raining.

JEREMY REED
January, 2018

To the memory of Hart Crane

Note

The 'Greenberg manuscript', a body of poetry written by a tubercular boy who died, at twenty three, in Manhattan State Hospital for the destitute, on Ward Island.

Did you ever see some of the hobbling yet really gorgeous attempts that boy made without any education or time except when he became confined to a cot? No grammar, nor spelling, and scarcely any form, but a quality that is unspeakably eerie and the most convincing gusto.
—Hart Crane in a letter to Gorham Munson

Distal 1

Season of close. The carmine thawfrost numbs
the excitation of such calentures
as fixture gulls into the wind's blueclimb,
outposting the tubercular
in a State Hospital on Ward Island.
A congealed crimson, then exstase issue,
inducts my febrilely posthumous hand
to engender notebooks of imagery.
Dying pricks with snow's sensitivity
on Manhattan's needlepoint mercury

'Unschizophrenic only in writing
                              my lung
resuscitates, restirs the green whirlpool
where the drowned oscillate on current-wings,
electrified by a scarlet systole
synonymous of depth-clairvoyancy -
a white hand immersive in memory.
Who rises, becomes nerve, reclaimed by sea.

Flotant to orientate anatomy,
invest your reliving this diary,
I fuel some brain explosure's aqualung,
and filter blood through a storm's instamat

of a white skin stripped from a persian cat
deluded by water's blue riffled string,

                                   as now,

from Manhattan Harbour a winch cable

                                               steals gear,

I re-instate your new writing-table.'

2 First Entry   Blue Snow after half a century

The floor's green-tiled. Zeroic cold-storage
depilates the fellic rigor-mortis
of bodies enveloped in apron-smocks –
a percolation of fugitive age
amplified to a quill's fibrillous timbre
in a metronome's oxygenized rondure.
Blue denims, a brandyflask, astrakhan snowcoat
attire my rising, as rift-wind, scuffed smoke
dropscreams from the evacuative wake
of a ship's riposte to the estuary.
A sealed letter awaits in secrecy.

                    '*Orizaba*.
– an acute arteriosclerosis
generates to a migraine nucleus
nodal in the glastonbury-blue tide
exscinding the white feelers of a head
dichotomously viewed, by hands reclaimed
from shadow hands around a bottle-neck –
hours without sleep, and the engine-room's tack –
a nihilistic ideation;
                    sixteen
years Stern outlived. Your opening, the respite
between asphyxiation and white throat.

Pseudonymous reassume a name,
the words compressed between the rail and stern.

Hart Crane'

3 'Terror of the irreversible or terror of the commitment . . .' Stern

Those seacloud whites, a paperpadded cell,
the sequence nevernone the black returns
to diffuse imagery, a punctured bell
dispersing sumac-billed black razorbills
stuttering on a magnifying-glass
in motion on what's irreversible.
Commitment is the writing table,
conspicuous with its blue typewriter.
And telepathic from a latent ribbon
round light, my isothermal snow finger.

                          (Outdawn
blacklight. Homunculi
tartan-capped on Manhattan scaffolding
space lights assertive of my foetion.
My wristseams blued with venous insulin,
mauve-tinted glasses, the air's fish-hawk
                              sting
finding the lung...
                 haemorrhage retrospect,
as much as emblems of conduct, recast.)

To find the right phrase from this aquacade
of cerebro-inversions. Past
revived, outlives, nullifies the future
poised in haruspicating electrodes
to startle words
in wake of the petrel's visionary stare.

4 Approaches

Awakening through neuronic zodiacs
through red and out of scotodinia,
reflective is my occipital track
                              my coming
to, presumptive of schizogenesis.
Motifed to my denims an identity disc
inscribes my isthmus-block, propensity
to write. Unoccupation – poetry.
In red letters the word *respiratory*.

'My mind hums to whatever dictates course.
This passage of colour
shearwaters concentrate in their outclimb
downcloud. But a retiary interior
discloses two left hands strapped to a wire,
intuitive with misgenerated fire,
raised red against a zinc compression-door.
Approaches to failure recharge the mind.
The space inside refaces a new sound.

I may outlive to rewrite my first death,
a death on approbation. Life inclines
that the re-stimulation of my brain

evaporate blood into poetry –

                              a sky
electric as the lizard-pink of dawn,
as outlined on some liner's snakeringed stream,
I pace the apartment's muffled heating,
daring to trespass on an escape-rung.
Learning to retrace cavities of pain.'

5 Scansion

The flat's retentive of such possessions
as immure a writer from homicide.
The doorhandle opening to a pistol,
gas-mask and flying-jacket, each stray bell
unreprieved by violence. A distant sun
less bright than the leather-tanned smog-neon
becomes retractive and in outgoing
                                    line-thin
and unterrestrial. No footfall rights
a car circuited and unwalked street.

        (distends to the sonar of a black cat
        machete skinned on an undertaker's floor
        nine lives further than a suspect future

my first, extemporised, nervous entry.)
Nervous in moves as the veneer relay
in disengaging the mind from tweezers
                                    blueway
of hands that probe.

        (breakfast unserved synonymous of that
        lycanthropic squeal from another door,
        steel-traces tightened, a susurrant switch

baring a brain-tumour's ensconced tissue.)
From each partition a car-light floods through,
if he should jerk, the incision...
revolves circumambiently the block
in a series of simulated stalls,
the coma releases perspiration...
exhaust-pipes open   jet-searing the walls,
the acceleration buzzing with fear;
irrevocable the precarious drill

                                    slips

on the bloodlight out...

                        (impaired, recourse is to a basement room

                        the cat

spits red round a telescopic Sten gun.)

6 Album

Glancing at mallards on the audient snow
lights in my tangible peninsula.
                              Placoid,
surf sleeted. On fog elevations below,
plexiglass, serum, fix the retina
from sprinting the eyewhites. If to avoid
crippled dimensions of the human mind
one courses the elevator's white-suede
interior inclimb,
a needle pricks the mind from black to wax to sound.

(A tuxedo, steel-glasses, hip-holster
and aerosol of ether table laid,
become in writing a seasmoke-retreat,
guillemot-cragged, cloud orange gap.

)Recapitulate
                    anthologies. Auden, and Allen Tate
                    allowed my coloured sand posterity.
                    Such segments arc of death of desuetude
                    intimate to my cells new poetry
                    contrafissured
                    from incompatibilities from solitude(

'Either way, thinking is expenditure
of energy better rephrased in words,
or water
weaving webbed wake-V's. An ephemeral
tenure insists that my anxiety
to exist inducts creativity.

Strapped to a lamp an artificial hand
rounds
interminably a tape-recorder's spool.

                Listen.
A ferry-saloon intuits across
the harbour-wake to a nearby ravine,
the backwash through fog adding impulse
                        to
my escapism
as whose drowned face resurfaces to strain?'

7 Shaping

With surgical attentiveness the theme
incipient evolves from IX. Observations
stand the seville-orange oval mirror
in psychopathic salvos of terror
at the spring-soled basketball-boots that run
to amplified drugstores, the cardiogram
unplugged, blue with vascular declension
'skinscooptock skiptock' –
no take-up.
A red stretcher and microphonic shout.

'I see mostly the books are paperbound
in psychedelia. Their patterns trace
something indiscernible in the mind,
almost the starting point behind a face
that reading, disappeared.
An ambulance screened-in the armchair's space.

All is mutative. Atrabilious.
Behind the sycophantic features strut
a blotting-paper-grey cardboard cut-out
of nihilistic metamorphosis.
An outboard motor trolleying blue wash
invests of reservation a retreat.

Words in the whirlpool posit barriers,
a clouded inverse circle. A chapter
unblanks. The contrast is the peninsula.'

8 Reconnaissance

All day, the air's kitten-resilient,
tonic with cormorants and racing-green.
(The chapter forming.) In realism
a voyeur uncircumspectly erects
a nylon-ladder   and with lenitude
faces the glass, while his rear pockets
are searched by police whose position elects
an unimpeded skylight altitude.

                                My island recess
becomes therapeutic,
a focal solitude.

'Suppose I simulated death, five years.
Left my eclectic manuscripts to fray
with a cigar-black literacy-executor,
dissolved into paper partition-walls

                              to
re-write, all would remain uncollected.
An unwritten   amnesiac moth-hole

                                     through
words   chrysaloid, discarded, cell-
shells, an ink invisible interior.

So many disappear into seasmoke,
a grey on grey outgoing. Sea terns drop,
squat, squawk and scutter on a blue wharf step
where floats,
the ultimate perspective of a book.

Z.49. Plum-black and block below,
the wind riffles the mesh of suicide-nets
tenaciously tabbied with a wild cat
contracted to a ginger abdomen.
My stay is transitory, Television,
a scarlet gunslinger erect to rape,
chalk window signs on my not going out…
                                        The threat
of a white chromium hearse is cyclical.

'My going is the chapter's inception –
simply the silence of water away
a disused boathouse and its spiral stair,
release from manumission, the kiosk
where a nude negro bares her
parted thighs…
Against such robotism, the waters
have a constant way.'
                        The move from
Manhattan
is more   mutations of identity.
Asleep, in-red-in-green punctured neon,
with skin vestiges of transvestism.

... Salem green bands, menthol,
cocaine is-GAS-diet
for carcinogenesis, death
is a
black cap worn in basket-ball.

(The move and chapter likewise impending.
In I, evolve induce
so diffuse a
persona

that words become a blue gulf devoid
                         of a bridge.
The cross-descent is a fomenting ridge.)

10 On the Move...

Glassbell years   gagged beneath an ethercone
(the taxidermist pinching claret-snuff
a parrot throbbing on amphetamines
                                                    lime-
rabic.) Accentual in height, recess,
Grosz infiltrates into the subconscious,
depicting Manhattan Harbour's sea-beige.
Lights with my mind   climbing another age.

The bulb's anacathartic. Sherbet pink.
The polythene discharge an anaerobe.
And still the surgeon insists how in *Love*
& Fame,
Berryman vomited. So poems think.
Flashing white spotlights on a blacktip road.

In diagnosis   a doll's chinablue
contractile body composed round deadflies,
whispers that poetry's diabetes,
always requiring words for insulin.
Words to temper the mind's anabasis
fed through an eye-dropper
of strain. Narcotics or a fixed trigger.
My phrase requires environmental change.

The bedside-unit opens to reveal
Life Magazine. (The year of desuetude.)
A mounted skull beneath a police-helmet,
the sutures sprayed in aerosol scarlet.
And Marilyn beside a pool...

                                 the towel

discarded,
as now my isthmus blues beyond the rail.

The Isthmus/ 5 Intakes

'Right down in the far right-hand corner, in the half-shadow, I thought I caught sight of a railwayman in a peaked cap vanishing through a door, as though terrified. Then suddenly a woman's voice, piercing and violent as a gunshot…'

From *Catastrophe* by Dino Buzzati

11 Intake 1

The ocean's luminous grandfather clock
                                        birds round
in sempiternal migrancy, fluffs wash
on ganoids of the boat's dinner-knife-wake,
                                        slow quacks
blackbacking, washed.
One perspex, plexiglass, herring-grey shed
awaits arrival. No inhabitants.
A helicopter's telescopic lens
at recurrent intervals   warns
of my sole, poetic-experiments.

A furry puttering on the elevated
                                        patio
disturbs.
                    The mentor is a gull without a head.
Cerebral-juice inseminated by
the friction of some cataleptic eye
with a viridian shark's voodoo-tooth,
screams with a red inaudible quiver
at the top of my sea-seat typewriter,
and responds to my own linguistic sonar.

                                    My mind follows
away from the scientist's quicklight globe.
Its mentor is a gull's head on an unmapped road.

12 Intake 2

My poem rounds an invisible spool
of tape replayed to the island mentor;
conserved from all periodic-journals,
reserved their rejection. Cod-spray rockpools
erratic in their flyblue brilliance,

                              punt seamews
into an automatic ball-
point precision. The linguistics are
erasable   then retraced on the water through
a cartridge   concealed in a gull's eye.

'If only someone would resuscitate
Harry Crosby, re-instate my right eye
in Hart Crane's left, revivify tonic
rhetoric...
but this anamorphosis of the

                              tape
is alien to my project   to project
syllabic asterisks from a severed gull's head,
experimental as the nervous red
positioned-lens   relayed to publishers.
Dichotomous as my renewed consciousness.
To Ward Island my existence remains untraced
in a necropolis   now posthumous.'

Words-flight and structure   is subliminal,
or inverted   the action is not time,
as restrictions impose. Seated in this
                              deck-chair,
my scalp perspicuous, devoid of hair,
a tightening of the light reveals a line.

13 Intake 3

Denuded as a photographic plate,
a diver threads on thermal quicksilver
asphyxiated   motioning a wake
of gyroscopic surveillance.
                              Inside,
the poems accumulate on blank scripts,
as lights follow a seal's shoal-crimson streak…

'Reversed, the spools record such history
as waters in this unmanned promontory,
ionized now by radar-hurricanes
the beacons
red blue cybernetics of a haemorrhaged brain
gyral on jet-hachures or flight tension –

Recluses shored this sand in empathy
the nervation of curlew-turquoise sky
appropriated runes.   The stupration
of reds   in   rite   as & now a kid-skinned
                              police mask
penetrates an addict in Manhattan,
analphabet, apart from an argot
                  of 'acid speed',
turned vomiting toward a goggled head.

The gull screams in its sensory, psychic-scare.
My binoculars reverse this ritual air.
The isthmus burns into a mullet-scale,
dogrose from despotism, but offshore
a white suit thins along a glass handrail
almost human   and in its coming fear.'

14 Intake 4

Blue hours to walk around the table round
the stratosphere of linguistics in
sand's orange-metabolism of sound
in resonance of a telephone's hum,
submersive, but alert.
                                 Fall migrants infraction
on my ionospheric wasp-live brain,
that even retreating to a sub-room
animates green bottles   my diary kept
in observing the gull's blood-feeding tract;
and a collapsible white suit's station.

Entry

Irascible the poem evolves from
the irritation of misconception,
energy generated in the search
for a word's eye, a black anatomy
of form,
inclusion and exclusion pared, the eye
asserting its approach.
Alert,
as though a gull's skylined quicksilver throat
the black imprint erased the white space quote.

Winter. The poems are congealed to waste
and outrun. Concealed through an iriscope,
distorting the nearness of a police-craft
my retreat
slipfingers through an intangible draft.

15 Intake 5

Each word proliferates in delusion
inside failure.   My chinese-heroin
and cabinet .45   placate megrims,
as sipping blood through a straw to fulfil
renewed respiration   I contemplate
the red horsehair torn from my sleeping cot.
In cyanosis my features duplicate.
Another's eyewhite makes the type-key fall.

My intake of rarefied green-oxygen
revivifies experimental drive.
Each day resuscitates how strange to live
undying from the migraines heart-tension
ills numerous that my transitory
lifelead would terminate should claws contrive
to startle my blood's perspicacity.

My contemplations should progress to chapters,
a need to supersede
the introspective. Psychedelia
hits in through quadrophonic neon lips,
pink hissing tapes that explode on water,
scouting black waves of some lysergic trip.
Manhattan floats in its neon transfer.

(Unpledge, prognosticate but know no depth
but dark   the motive to erase vestige,
clothes off, shoes and identity papers,
the letter left to calculate no age
of understanding.

                    Words I simulate,
hire an uptown apartment and retreat.)

16 Chapter: 'Forster's syndrome'

Rare bisociations with surgery

but known to

phylogenetic research.

Apex

subdued intonations

to ventricle,

hawkwind-held rift to rhythmic energy,

the toy-locomotive of imagery

rounding with a pastel nursery-rhyme

out-red and then the disappearing train.

Chloral hydrate and the normality.

Evocation

of green pitters becomes a leafless rain.

Inside the monotonous beat out, beat

red of blood heats vaguely to accelerate

to death. Strip-lighting, vapid movie-stars –

move open fishnet thighs above the cars

eroded with toxics, laning the slush

to throttle on a fogpole a gold thrush,

its features limp. Alive, malnutritive.

The traffic-lights become eyes that alive

search out apartments in flood wires of stripes.

Enlighten a saddler's-whip, cosmetic rape...
All burns. The air is mustard. Consumptive.

Awkward in nerve-ends a deaf apathy
causes intermittent paralysis.
Always the word behind the poem's eye
discloses to conceal. One life consumed,
I realize re-dying that the dead
are faces in the poem unconceived.
Are attributes inside no attached head.

17 Failure 2

Madison Avenue's sub-human void,
grouse-grey with cars, no foot would dare encroach,
anonymously mails my monthly blood
in enzymes of unbreakable test-tubes.
Mirrors accompany my walking through
electric points, the *Orizaba*'s stern –
depicted in a photograph album.
Suicide is so dark depth passes through.

Day, night, the hours are a venesection.
Exhaust filters green through respiration
and cramps the fingers to a whisky glass.
The typewriter remains hooded, stray script
drizzles into an encumbrance, vague draft
accentuating ennui then decline
into a thermometer's scarlet brain.
Writing to countenance my own failure,
I hear a rail decamped, stalled propeller...
(the eyes scansion to cruise back and
                              surrounded
the instant's overkick into blue space,
features contorted in downtreading depth,
compression racing through the lungs that seethe

in repetitious hallucination;

                            reface

in pyjamas from the drumming black stern

a switchback before the Caribbean

opened, disclosing once an upthrust arm.)

18 Failure 3

On slides, black monogram, red carnation –
the facsimile of my arts patron
admonishes my obtuse   strained failure
to electromagnetize   calligrams
from the noon-glare of the *Orizaba*'s stern.
The splayed-out paralysis   stunned-spiral
a pellet-vortex,
discharged through burns that swim inside the eye,
resurface through the vein of poetry.

Dusting his glasses in a hotel suite,
the patron features as illiterate,
his cinefilm is one of dollar notes.
His secretary is incurious
to the advance of his cheroot fingers,
and cobalt nails primed as a peacock's throat.
Nonchalantly he broods over a wordless tape
ocean-tracked   and views the iced-water tap.

In block 222 distant from his suite
my mind develops pictures of a creek,
demersal, punctuated by such tides
as colour energy with new language.

19 Failure 4

The personal world its introspective globe
inks in grey cramps of occlusion. Failure
of mind, the self stripped to denudation,
and then the surgery that life decodes
hands caught distraught as though still conducting
with an instrument of euthanasia
the toxic scarlets   of a frail tenure
                                        open
as eyewhites round an oven's nostril-ring.

'In six phases my self-immolation
(no deflated climax) cyanide-pin,
nor patient J.W. arguing
the merits of a red plastic dragon.
A simple withdrawal from self, language.
The hand's reversal to the obverse page.

Almost despaired of a forthcoming book
delayed blood signal to my indolence
displayed as retiary in retreat
of an imaginary review's suspense.
Potential in the rat whose helmet spins
outside the plexiglass features human

elastic strait jacket but no penis
to disseminate an impaired species.

Ovoid

to death and in the unbecoming range
Manhattan Harbour for the transferred word
alliterative with the genocide
of sensory response. Tired, pigeon-grey,
my cigarette ash ticks across the bay.

20 Nadir

Death's dread despair of ingested round fur,
an intestinal kitten-knot. Hotels
recriminate with bed-stained sheets, letters
addressed from self to self knife-seamed open,
a latent suicide note pasted on
a neon-placard.   Publishers postpone
incipient contracts as threadbare seams
expose underarm acid-yellow stains.
Blank manuscript inks in through carbon steam,
and out, an eyelash without a pupil.
Coincidental of a writer's fall

       to

       die sub-schizoid, feet turkey tucked and stitched
       tumescent with synthetic hormones, towelled
       into a locked nose-bleed, constipated

          through

       sealed orifices. Starched physical pain
       before the more mental degradation.

         Ever

       humiliation, the intent subsumed
       by words secreted to debase, acute in

         anger

       distemper. Ever an agitated

brilliance of sepia, friends turned against
or turning.
        Always the nose-notched bed-post
allows discomfiture, the derailed mind
        that stales
into the eyerun of its own features
and in its nylon nostrils no beyond
nor self dimorphic from suffocation,
        emerges.
'Almost ... and if I tried ... almost' the voice
audible, half-toned, then a snuffled scream
        that snaps.

21 Exit

Debentures, X-ray cards, surgical tape
                              accumulate
from white suede gloves no arms accounted for,
but the hum of an elevator's door,
and the pinpush of an armoured police-car
circuiting the block from dawn to dawn
no sky distinguished from the stripneon,
only red insulin significant.

'To rise, photostat one's rejection-slips,
and see reflected on the white skylight
a mongol with a trained albino rat
unfastening the suicide-net;
the tomato-juice rising to eject…
NO EXIT
flashed across the corridor's green instep.

It's more the atrabilious failure
of receptivity, failure to write,
or writing circulate.
                        No publisher
allows for dissonant experiment…
The clique tightens round gold-necked bottle tops,
casual at parties on luxury yachts,

tonal with dark glasses, affectation.
The features olive-deckled to reject
literature for a loose bikini-strap.
Bourbon follows.
                    No forthcoming contract.

More frequent now, my falling; accidents,
the scar reasserting itself aware
of blood-spots. And the imperturbable
biro inlined with a cartridge-razor.

22 Exit 2

The apartment contracts to a suitcase,
my writing credentials. A red bull's-eye
focussed on my bedboard focuses back
to an electronic anatomy.
                                    Unhinged
vandals deploy the building's fire-escape,
conducting mind-games on a pullman's track,
frog-thumb the windows, on ledges excrete…
incite exterior menace.
                                There's no retreat.
                            EXIT
swingdoors turn in upon themselves, then out
into a sheer two-hundred-storey drop
into a   hallucinatory foyer
where an electric funeral   scarlet cap
are compressed through a harmonica's wail.
                                        'And

let
subside the contract   and remote controlled
brain stitches from a Swiss neurologist,
allow air bubbles to circuit the wrist
rage out the stasis on a black-foam bed

and find suspension tortured on a shred
of sheet fibred inside the heart.'

                               Heights down,
ignition keys register rage. The man
with olive features disappears with script
and screams around a clinkered petrol can.

23 Exit 3

Pacing the carpet saucer-bald I float
in vapoured formalin about the room,
increase in velocity to a shout
stoking endermic burns.
                              'Hallucinate
Hart Crane and go, that likewise resuscitated,
as behind words as you were in advance
my infringement is of second failure.
Catbox-restricted with no desk-distance,
only the one   imaginary road
held by a simulated wheel   that speed
dictates to my inner balance.
                              The autodrive
is so intense my poems fibrillate,
discharge adrenalin   and offpage move.

The failure is the suffocation of language
a foot's shadow eclipsed by each new step,
a vague
surgical-pinkness lighting an image,
then depth.
In the end everything goes to the rat.
The poem beats inside a rodent's heart,
enters the yellow of hospital strokes

in the tongue's instant of paralysis…

                    The nurse
stripped, limp as an asphyxiated mouse,
unable to disentangle the noose,
and reach the insistent alarm exit.

24 Exit 4

No longer is the height below reprieve
but anger. Footsteps tick inside the hand
of a stopped watch and then circle surround
the heart's silent pacemaker. An orange
carlight becomes intentionally the sun
strapped to a microphonic-intrusion
of tapes repeatedly calling my name,
photographs produced as to so derange
estrangement.

        Painful self-intimacies exposed
the hand caught in masturbation
the simulated hairpiece   transfusion
and inner-lining of all digressions.

                       The grey
repository we recognize as sin.

        Fender to fender
locked ambulance wheels erase all exit,
white-coats armed with power-torches and nets
flicker red armbands and perambulate,
eyeslits through leather
masks, cleaver
and tether.   On the farscape
the handle opens into vertigo,
no floor in suspension above the street,

A megaphone enunciative,

bicephalic poet   *human cage*

as sheet by sheet torn manuscript

amalgamates with reds of ticker-tape.

25 Exit 5

Falling, the circle's always contracting
to an imaginary node. Right foot
in space, the left bird-hooked to scaffolding,
a viscous curlicue of nausea
entrailed in white ribbons about the throat,
fluorescently shell-bald, to leave swinging
a mannequin, and make an armed retreat
into the black pores of an oil cellar.

                              Dying
is not the extroversion envisaged,
but something pain withdraws to a subdued
release.
So rare the crisis that the lungs explode
like swiftly compressed riding fish.
Leaving total suspension, two red valves
paralysed by the pistol's butt;
while outward flashlights on the dummy hiss,
pitter, and jockey pigeons across street.

                             Secret
comminates secret. Death is abatement,
an arcana of privacy. Private
the flesh but not the manuscript.

                           Outside,
the crowd instigates, invokes suicide,

unaware indoors of a private stain,

                                    the basin

floating red string of a segmented brain.

Nov-Dec 1973

A Note from the Publisher

This volume is part of a series devoted to recovering out-of-print volumes that – in my view – should be made available again. The books date from the 1960s to the 2000s and many of them have been important to me in one way or another for a long time. All are out of print in their original form, although some can be found within their authors' subsequent collected editions.

The Isthmus of Samuel Greenberg was first published in a beautifully-designed and -printed edition of 526 copies in 1976 by the American poet-designer-printer, Asa Benveniste, at his Trigram Press in London. Trigram was one of three small presses that dominated the 'alternative' British poetry scene of the 1960s and early 1970s, the others being Stuart Montgomery's Fulcrum Press (which closed down in 1974) and Tom Raworth and Barry Hall's Goliard Press – later Cape Goliard Press after its acquisition by Jonathan Cape in 1967. All of them exhibited splendid design, all had poets at the helm, and they were all instrumental in bringing the 'New American' poets of the post-Beat generation, the New York School, and the Black Mountain poets to the British public, alongside non-mainstream British figures such as Roy Fisher, Gael Turnbull, Nathaniel Tarn, Lee Harwood, Tom Raworth, J.H. Prynne, Tom Pickard and Jeremy Reed. Sharp-eyed readers will note that five of that list have already appeared in Shearsman livery and another has had two Shearsman collections of essays devoted to his work.

This edition makes no pretence to the high production quality of the Trigram edition, but *Isthmus* deserves to be available in this *Shearsman Library* series: Jeremy has several later volumes on the Shearsman list; we're both Essex University alumni, and I've had a copy of the original edition of *Isthmus* since 1980. It's a book I've long liked despite its youthful excesses. Juvenilia? Perhaps, but Asa Benveniste was right about this one. Assorted typographical errors have been corrected, and it deserves to see the light of day again.

Tony Frazer,
January 2018

www.ingramcontent.com/pod-product-compliance
Lightning Source LLC
Chambersburg PA
CBHW020218090426
42734CB00008B/1119